Peppers

Lada Kratky

Photographs by

Fernando and Barbara Batista

HAMPTON-BROWN BOOKS

MANY CULTURES, MANY LANGUAGES...MANY POSSIBILITIES!™

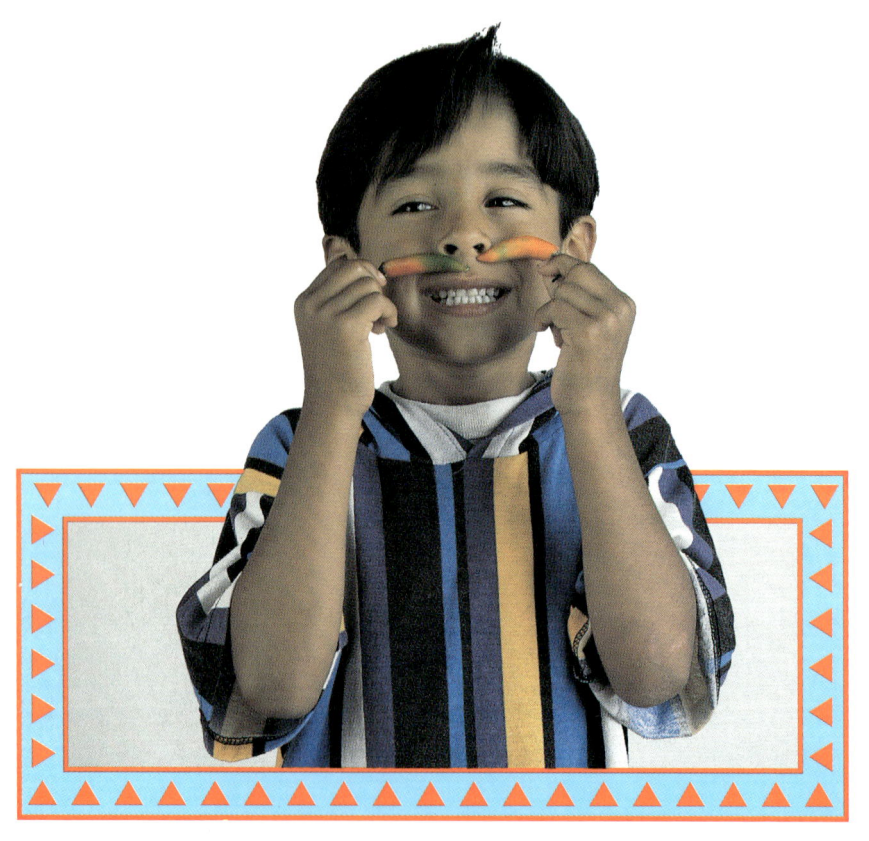

Make a mustache.

Make a beard.

Make the letter Z.

Make two eyes.

Make a face.

Make some salsa, please.

The salsa is the best of all.
Try some, and you'll see!